HERESWAY

Also by Sam Truitt

POETRY BOOKS

Dick: A Vertical Elegy (2014, Lunar Chandelier)
Vertical Elegies 6: Street Mete (2011, Station Hill)
Vertical Elegies: Three Works (2008, UDP)
Vertical Elegies 5: The Section (2004, Georgia)
Anamorphosis Eisenhower (1999, Lost Roads)
The Song of Rasputin (1996, Golden Books)
Blazon (1991, Deep Forest)

EDITED VOLUMES

Editor, with Michael Ruby. *Eating the Colors of a Lineup of Words: The Collected Early Books of Bernadette Mayer* (2015, Station Hill)

Editor, with Anne Gorrick. *In|Filtration: An Anthology of Innovative Poetry from New York's Hudson Valley* (2016, Station Hill)

AV SERIES

Dick (Oblique)
The Best of "Days"
shaft/state state/shaft
Transverse

HERESWAY
Vertical Elegies 10

Sam Truitt

MADHAT PRESS
ASHEVILLE, NORTH CAROLINA

MadHat Press
MadHat Incorporated
PO Box 8364, Asheville, NC 28814

Some of these works appeared, sometimes in earlier versions, in the following publications: *Apogee; Chronogram; Colorado Review; Devouring the Green: Fear of a Human Planet: An Anthology of New Writing,* ed. Sam Witt (Jaded Ibis Press, 2015); *Fence; Gianthology; Ping-Pong: A Literary Journal of the Henry Miller Library;* and *Plume.*

The Library of Congress has assigned
this edition a Control Number of
2018936383

ISBN 978-1-941196-68-7 (paperback)

Cover image: *Mexia* (2016), acrylic and charcoal
on canvas, 58″ x 48″, by Kimberly Truitt
Cover design by Marc Vincenz
Book design by MadHat Press

www.madhat-press.com

First Printing

To the memories of Andre and Vala Enard, Ernest Bradley
& C.D. Wright, in perfect brilliant stillness

Table of Contents

Reality is that which, when you stop believing in it, doesn't go away.
—PHILIP K. DICK, *I Hope I Shall Arrive Soon*

… all together, one, continuous … everything is full of what is …
—PARMENIDES, from "Fragment 8"

We were born naked, and everything else is drag.
—RUPAUL, variously

I

The soul is the seed
of destruction

inviting you
here pilgrim

in the light of
this crooked

lantern hung
between heaven

& hell as dusk
breathes in the mountain

& I step into
this forest echoing

what lipsings
what can't be

heard but
hears thru all

its branches at
the end of all

these identities
nothing is real

II

To throw our arms
around a moment

throws our arms
around the dream

enveloping
the universe we

are the voice
of throbbing

III

There is music
in the woods

——

something burning

in the cave

——

something singing
us breathes in

stillness the key
the edge of

which is this
sound one

connects once
one abandons

what one once
heard let

go to know

——

all we
are a form of

——

open

IV

The way escapes
no dance

& calling to
its rhythm

our hearts open
in its prism

flows in every
direction every

dimension
there is joy

& there is each
moment met

in surrender
to its swarm

V

I want to be
real to the ground

that's left me
to tender

listening
thru ribs of Earth

to the mouth
to the cave

to the darkness
inside me

leaping out
of the way

VI

Time may stop
in any direction

another dimension
psyche is waiting

against a wall
on which a life

is painted
to happen

—

in silence

indescribable
inexpressible

as words fall
only ahead of

what cannot
escape

—

a breath

VII

From one
to another

to another
to another

mouth opens
the world we

find we
rest in

the nature of
rhyme is

the end
of time

VIII

Solar Maximus

I am seconds away
from you

from me
from anything

we can discover
or describe

or strike a chord
against

like a colossus
waiting in our form

to find us

IX

There's a dot
of gasoline

in each of our
eyes a rainbow

that flickers when
we open them to

the light the dead
see out of

time
    & it falls
across this

page this
throb no

moment can hold
the end

of open

X

We can tell the shape
of a person's head

by the sound of the voice
coming out of it

—

but what about the dead

—

or our own spread-

eagle on the raft
of speech before

the silence of
no rogue wave

on no ocean
we can name

ourselves &
know we know

no more than
letting go

XI

Silence the house
dwelling in it

the house silence
forms in it

formlessnesses
of stone passing

thru us
        —a breath
bodies   unearth

XII

Our lives face
& are the face

of a cliff we
awake on &

on climbing
out of space

the blueprint
a breath took

in at birth &
never let

know—we don't
know—we

really don't
know only

go

XIII

Under the dome
of the assassin

my ass in
the air eating

the numbers
that encircle

your clitoris
that is the mother

of god I feel
my life pitch

back & where
it was

is a house
of dreams

XIV

The Sun

Things made
without love

turn out
the same

identical
to the task

—

but to make

love one
is flung

beyond creation

XV

I'm going to rig
up some words

here to climb
the scaffold

to the last thing
alive to sing

of nothing
to no one

with nowhere
to be

XVI

It might well be
there are kinds

of cold no
heat can touch

—no rhythm
heal—no one

know—no
holes it enters

& cannot
escape surrender

to the music

XVII

There there
is no there

to turn to
in the dream

to talk to
you of a face

exiting time
—

the coyote howls
—in the meat

& ruin &
ravishment rhyme

hides behind
& before the heart

can beat there
laughing there

signing singing
—

there is nowhere
inside no center

staring out
no crater at

the edge of what
I am I am

passing thru

XVIII

We walk echoing
in our hearts

the surface of
the sun &

so can't
see in the sky

where we are
our image

concealed
calling us

to listen
once

XIX

For a wee
while a wee

light burns in
a cabin in

the universe music
comes from

—

that ways of

life surround
—

that a being
may fly past

the sun—naming
stars with

fire with
which we are—

one
    invisible
spark

XX

With dead hands
I lift the dead

words spill
from images

XXI

To the balls   of my feet
to the brick   of my loins

the song   of my heart
—

to everything
I carry—the meat

of my consciousness
weighs nothing

more than what
nature's face

leaps out

XXII

I want to say
more than is

near & stay
here within

a world to
measure

—

without spinning

or waving my arms
like a bird

on a bough bouncing
up & down

—

& still somehow
touch my tongue

to the riddle
in the middle

of the rose love
ruthfully codes

—

organizing a shadow

in the shadow
of the sun

XXIII

Open The Rainbow

We are alone
in the world

—we are naked
to our world

—we are nothing
of this world

that can be
named only

broken

desires flashing
on & off   in

& out of us
like stardust

& everything we touch
here burns

XXIV

To see my dog
in real time drink

from a stream
in the mountains

under a purple
sky his focus

like a needle
on a needle

balancing
point to

point so
clear you can't

even see it
wobbling

a breath
lets go

a way out

XXV

Nothing real
can happen more

than once

XXVI

At last the magic's
not what can be

found but make
of our star our

first tongue
—first hominid

—first whisper
—

inside idiom
like a garden

gnome calling
us home

—*eaht*

XXVII

Just this
then then

to begin again
when nothing

is separate is
here at all

I want to know

XXVIII

When I see
an open box-

car door I grow
horns & wings

—

& write in

no tense in
no thing in

no time that
is beautiful

& real looking
far away

from here
for the way

wove around
what speaks

to Ishtar's
lonely world

—

adonai

XXIX

A perfect evening
—

a shadow of
a tree on

the wall is
writing—to

sit inside &
grow still

enough to
climb to

put words in
place of

—

XXX

Earth swallows
flesh swallows

life swallows
breath

—

& there is no

escape we
can make that

doesn't fit in
our mouths

miracles

XXXI

These words
in lines are

placed the way
fire stares

thru our faces
—

branches
—

forests
—

worlds on
fire—fanning

darkness

XXXII

To begin
think

into a ring
everything

that's ever
been &

then escape
nothing

XXXIII

The real world
is right here

in the face
of a book

open to
itself

XXXIV

There's a light
coming out of

my head called
words alone

on this road
to guide me

open before
my eyes find

a knot fate
left tied to

nothing I
can say a

breath away
from love

XXXV

At each bit
end at the end

of each twig
end at the end

of all the branches
live or dead

of this tree
is a star

if we look up
thru a breath

we feel sway
at its heart

XXXVI

Myth   the riff
mind   the rhyme

in the throne
room time

—

in a sunshine

of thieves
—

the crystals
of love

—

to ride to

the end where
no thing alone

dangles in
the throb words

flow from here
—

eternally blowing
out the stars

XXXVII

In stiff   cat-world
kabuki   Calliope

gone thru the fence
sits in a neighbor's

yard to wait
for Elsie to

emerge & play &
it's rained but

it's just wet
& quiet now

& unendlessly
bit by bit

the world burbling
ungroans on

a short-handle
shovel b/w

a hole & heap
singing the stump

of once

XXXVIII

The story is
as old as one

moment ago
the coyote is

howling across
the lake geese

start into the dark
like a rope of

sound flung
overhead as

long as you hang
from what balances

a blade the edge
of which is one

question you
have life to

touch—
        arched
back head
           aflame—

asking   nothing
that can be
           named

XXXIX

Her coast

—

it's impossible
to measure

—

there is no

way to get
there

—

you can only

get there

—

from here

XL

I'm going to sit
on my ass

& speak into
your face what

comes to me
from behind

watching a sound
being formed

from a message
being tore

out of the love
letters breathed

into my heart
to fling back

the dark
world we leave

together

XLI

Sunset approaching
along a dark path

I have tried to love
or not to hate

the best I can
to put in words

works in all
directions lines

of sight sound
binds & touch

nears b/w
the trees
            a knot

of light blinks
here

XLII

This is the dead
of winter

silence
on a stake

at the edge of
some woods

across a field
of snow these

lines fall
in place of

staring
thru hollow eyes

on mortality

XLIII

The poem is
a microcosm

of space like
something missing

because it's not
there or a lover

turns to see
getting up in

the mirror
afternoon sun

unmade together
chest rising

& falling in
copper light

that's never been
opened it

is the secret
that must be met

XLIV

The Caress

There's a tail
like a comet's

behind the sun
we are wove

to like one
braid of fire

with our planets
we ride together

with our breath
turns & every

woven thing that
moves between

us space is
energy on

a journey
we have only

begun to
be

XLV

The dream is clear
as a field of

rows of mown
hay like symmetrical

ripples
—

my dog ahead
standing watching

a man standing
in a field writing

no distance
away as the sun

sinks but incredibly
bright because

of how clear it is

XLVI

I have to slow e-
nough to let the

information catch
up with walking

drunk holding
myself up from

the sealed door
—

as though there
were one road

other than here
darker than alone

in rhythms of
power & trust in

rhymes with dust
& fire the shape

of an owl at
the start of calling

the forest to wrap
itself around what

is swarming
—

song

XLVII

Both answer &
a question we

stare in the end
into a prism

that has no edge
we can come to

or leave
in no time

unmoving
departing

what dreams

XLVIII

This Place Is Here For You

At the entrance
to my rhythm

is a wilderness
of mirrors in

place of words in
place of sound like

2 mountains in
place of myself

kissing the ground
& a rough patch

of road to nowhere
as can be found

in the space of
beginning before

we have begun
in place of eyes

to touch the rain
no rhyme swallows

like the sun

XLIX

I know the name
of man is mud

because I've held
his hand & hauled

his bucket & ate
& drank the crescent

moon of this life
taking hold of

nothing there the
last we breathe

Earth

L   **Elsewhere**

The tendency
of nature is

to flower as
silence is to

soul a breath
away from life

the heart is
in flight thru

my chest out
which spark

the sound of
the moon I

call thought
to witness now

sway

LI

Inherently the hand
is tragic lying

like a mask or
thru treetops

the wind in
the darkness

I form around
my words in

what dust in-
tones around

us no name
in no hieroglyphics

stars frame
eyes open

face a breath
away waiting

to shatter

LII

I am one that
seeks to enter

no place in
every direction

rhyme itself
hides in hands

open touching
no distance

—

where there is no

turning back

—

or aside—or
at all points

to the prism
we sing at

every throb
we leave together

LIII

Our bodies form
a secret none

knows the end
of shaped like

a pearl nobody
can find to sound

its opening out
which means

we hear it
hold our seed

in the moment
our lives give

birth to the sun
& we will be

forever sung

LIV

The land of the dead
is the oldest country

—

 it alone

cannot be wrought
mathematically

—

but wherever we

are it carves
how the sun

sings   what
never   darkens

LV

We have to come
to the end of the road

to feel the ground
at the end of the climb

give up its ghost
arranging some dust

at the end of time
—

to know one rhyme
breathe into each

other each
other each

speck we speak
—

to gather what
we are & have

made of   bounding
off a building

of shadows

LVI

If you watch you
can see stars move

in a sphere
—

like the sun
like Earth like

all things like
ourselves groove

scaling a spiral
stair auguring

out enough to
mask the void

I feel dangle
like ash at

the end of
a breath

—

a breath

LVII

It's been a pleasure
serving you

cosmos
in my branching

way aching
of the heart

cut out of what
I haven't

found &
swallowed

to keep you
here to sound

the form our
mouths open

in absence

LVIII

We search
for the unlit

sun when
there is none

to wave in
front of dust

the last sign
of mind

vs. rhyme
vs. hole

we find
staring at

the end of
this derangement

our lives face
out
    Lucy

is alive

LIX

Once there ran
in the forest

—

to the east

it ran
—

to the west
—

south
—

north
—

there was no
place it did

not go thru
the heart of

Prometheus in
place of words

in place of
us in place

of what is
& there was

fire

LX

Look   at the house
—

it looks real
—

ropes & pools of
light along the 8-

inch each mile
curve of Earth swept

in an arc—it
is impossible

to conceive of
another 1000

years of this
unless sung

—

the way our words

coil around
a tree planted

in the dark
& where we are

speech & dust

LXI

Just a face
—

nothing
to describe

disguise
or add to

the terror of
—

looking out
at it

of it
—

the unknown

LXII

The invisible pyramid
over Cooper Lake

glints in the moon
light to line

up under the mind
of Orion the world

opens to touch

LXIII

Welcome to my song
ground of groin

whittled whistled
hole with open

eye
—

welcome to nothing
—

welcome to leg
thrown over fence

no thought
follows what

dangles here
compressed

—

to hang in

face what
words express

LXIV

A Mosaic Of Waving

I'll learn to read
the world in lines

radiating
rhyme until

I find the one
I sway on

the tip of
on on &

climb into this
breath without

leaving time
to lock a leg

over the neck
of a house

fly & let
go the trembling

sky wandering
in a maze of eyes

picking b/w waves
of light the lint

out of my navel
without hands

LXV

When we let
go the mind

we let
go the rhyme

let go long
ago to hide

what we can't
find when we

close our eyes
we're not leaving

for we've no
place to go

all things show
thru the open

chord our form
mouths in silence

drifting home

LXVI

To storm the open
start in the head

a wave of wind
on the ocean

of what is said
to sway in

the middle of
the house in

a center of
air at the hub

of a wheel in
the raw place

behind the eyes
I call psyche

sunk deep in
the meat of

the sun in
asylum affixed

to each breath
as a model of

the universe at
rest is boundless

dangling over the cliff
edge   the heart

finds   silence
looks out

LXVII

Shoot limbs
out in either

direction &
reach in

neither you
sway axis

of what cannot
outlast a

breath atlas
of what is

LXVIII

Write it down
& it is gone

but it is less
gone the sun

a knot b/w
2 trees the moon

a page camped
on our trail &

died to fling
above the green

a grid the wind
swallows in

a forest room
to bend what

spacetime we
sing spherical

LXIX

I've aligned
the face a

hurricane made
of wind &

scope &
object of

desire called
my life to

ripple here
in the lost

order shelter
shatters as

there is no
other no

place to get
to to hide

what I am
swaying keep

blowing against
the horn of

a unicorn on
acid twisting

whorls thru lines
into the dark

world we leave
gleaning nothing

to form no limit
to rhyme or hold

to take gyre to
touch words lips

LXX

I wonder how
things are

in the precinct
sleep hides

before auguring
the dream I

speak out to
hold open or

let go closed
in a mirror

—

on a cliff

—

its mouth

—

a breath

LXXI

The Monolith

A dog fetching
a ball our lives

go out &
come back to us

like a breath
on a hill

above a river
no bridge no

one crossing
can hold forever

LXXII

I want to be
the moment I

was made out
of a cloud of

dust wrapping
my arms around

the desire I
came from

—

& hear still

on a street
corner
    —waiting

—balancing my
load
    —wet with

rain
    —the thunder
shudder no name

LXXIII

There's a question
mark in

reverse at
the edge of

the white
woods the weight

of words as
far as sight

& no sound on
hemlock boughs

allow hung
here at the tree

line the universe
leaves signs

howl *howl*
—

LXXIV

Everything
I used to know

about the structure
of clouds draws

near to take
the shape a maple

leaf on a branch
of a tree of them

humming the green
rhythm a stand

holds forms hands
waving the song's

one breath

LXXV

To stick a stick
in the ground

is to stake
the world

or sway in
the arms of

a tree almost
alive as no

human is
to another

human &
silence

looking out
a sky on

a star we
can never know

the end of
beginning

LXXVI

The way is
the way

either a nerve
or a vein

open the poem
is a prism

as Earth's
breath so

for all I seek
to make it

glow my mind
is not my home

or own or
what's said

psyche leaves
to breathe in

song

LXXVII

In the middle of things
—

the eye that
can't be seen

in the middle
of things darting

flame in the middle
—

dancing to dust
the moment Earth

looks away from us

Index of Titles or First Lines

About the Author

Sᴀᴍ Tʀᴜɪᴛᴛ was born in Washington, DC, and raised there and in Tokyo, Japan. He is the author of the ten books in the Vertical Elegies series, among other works in print and other media. He has received grants and awards from, among others, the Howard Fellowship, the Fund for Poetry, and the University of Georgia. Robert Creeley likened Truitt to "a contemporary Everyman." The President of the Institute for Publishing Arts and Director of Station Hill Press, he lives in Woodstock, NY. For more: samtruitt.org.

www.ingramcontent.com/pod-product-compliance
Lightning Source LLC
Chambersburg PA
CBHW022013080426
42733CB00007B/588